To My Sweetheart and My Kids

Original comic & story developed by Travis Hanson
Adopted from the Novel Bean Song by Travis Hanson & Aimee Duncan

For contact information, subscription or letters to the artist, please send all inquiries to
Bean Leaf Press
P.O. Box 6495
Moreno Valley CA 92554

Softcover ISBN 978-1-4507-9715-3

Printed in USA

the BEAN

Volume One: Riddles and Shrooms

Travis Hanson

www.beanleafpress.com

Riddles
& Shrooms

Shrewd Bargainings

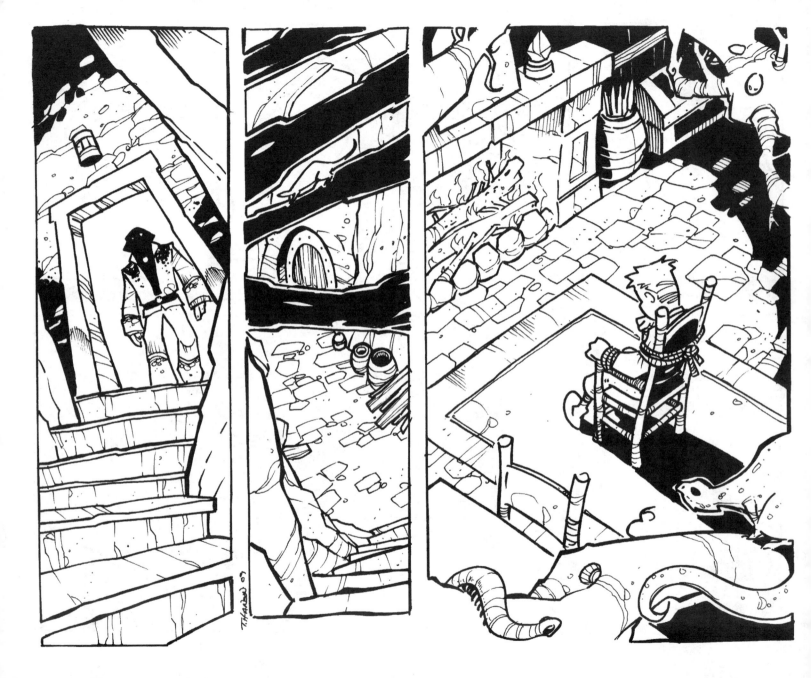

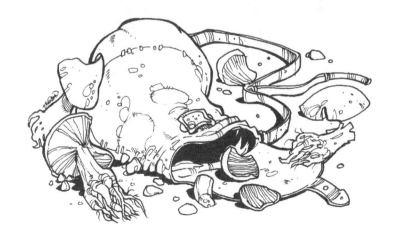

Into the Dark

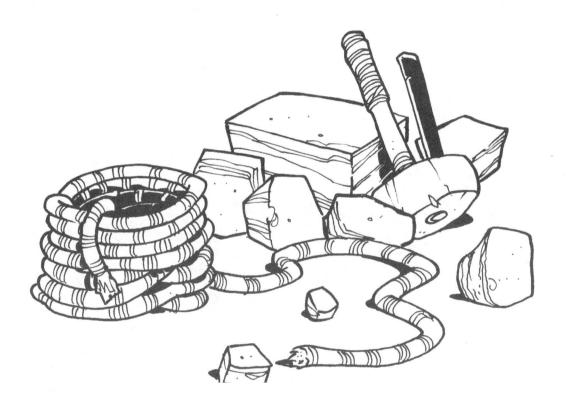

SORRY, BEAN,

FINDING YOU WILL HAVE TO WAIT.

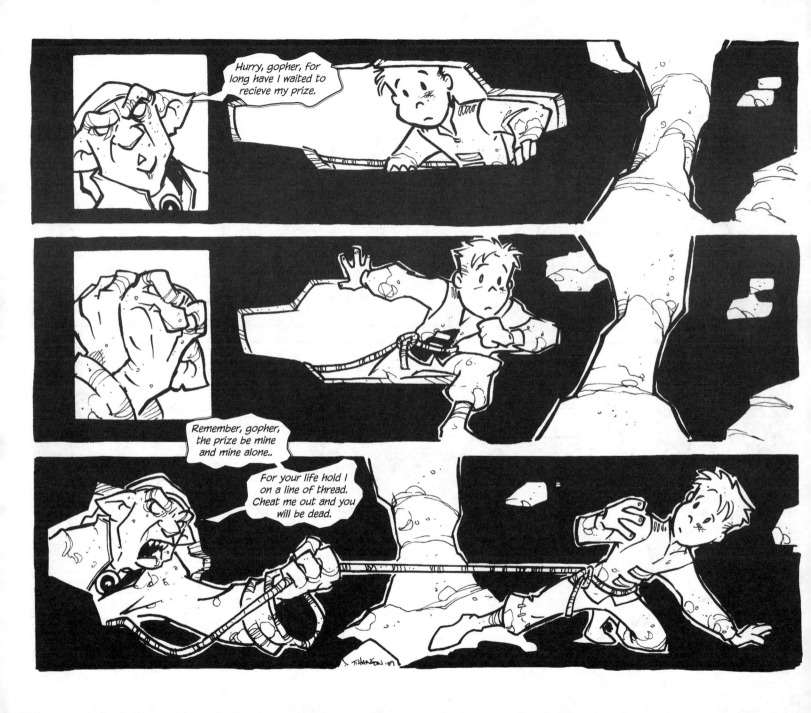

Forgotten Stories

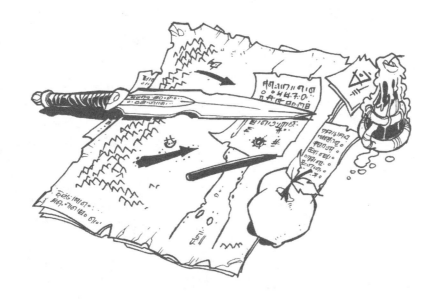

KA-BOOM!

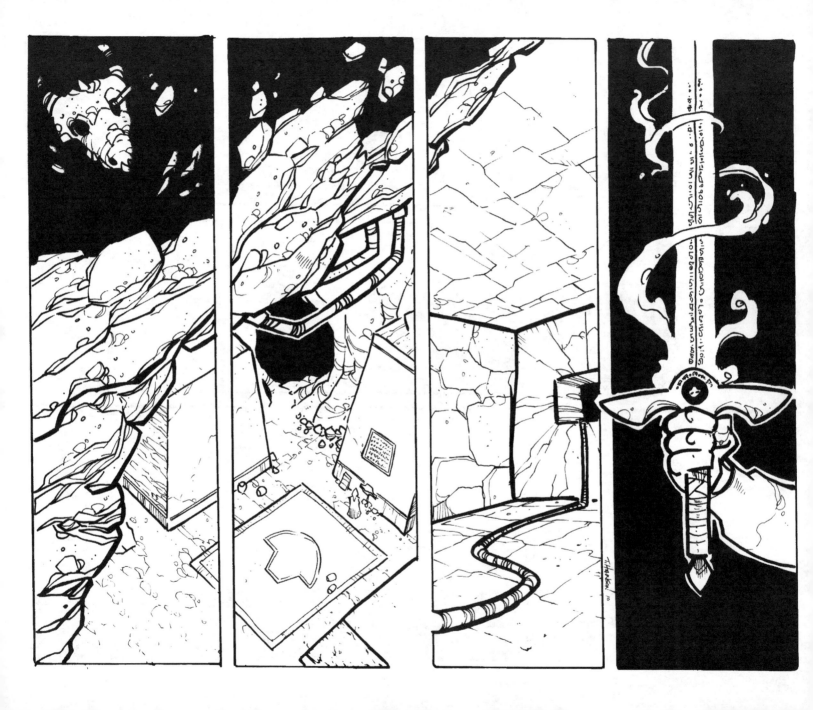

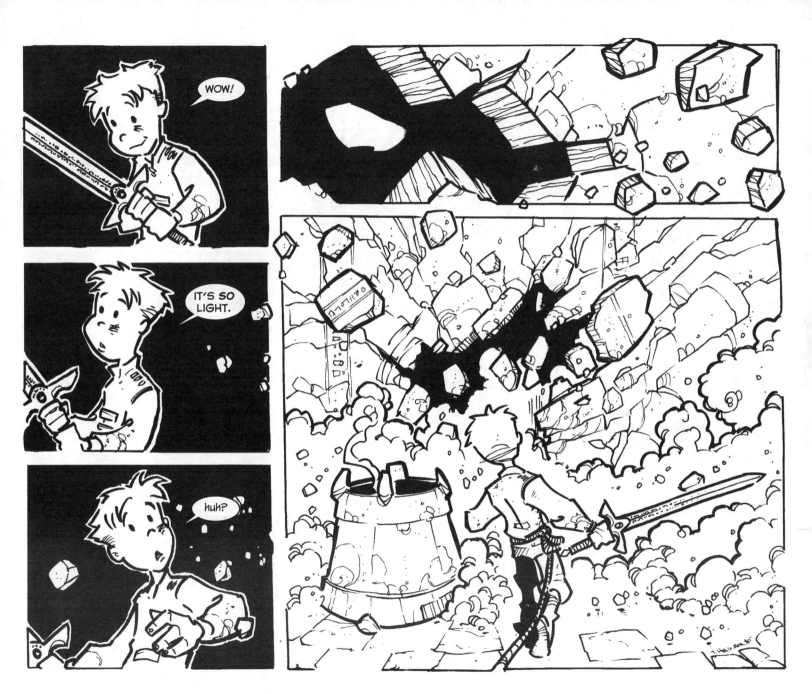

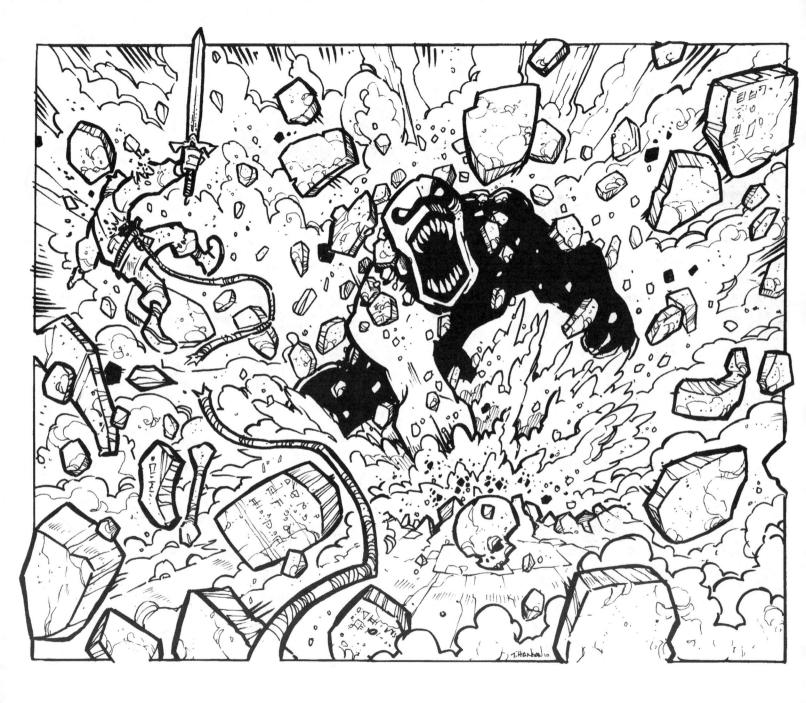

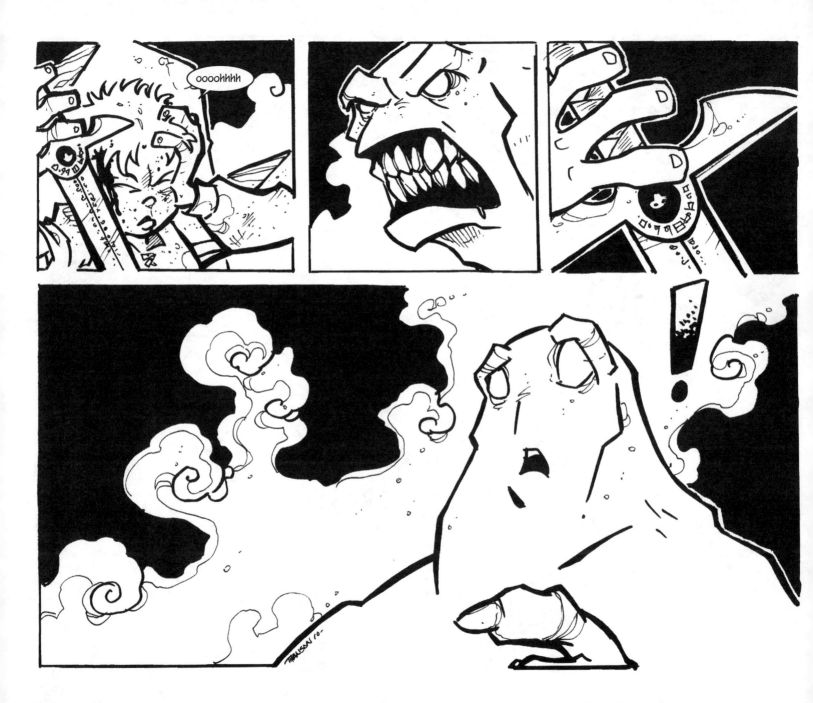

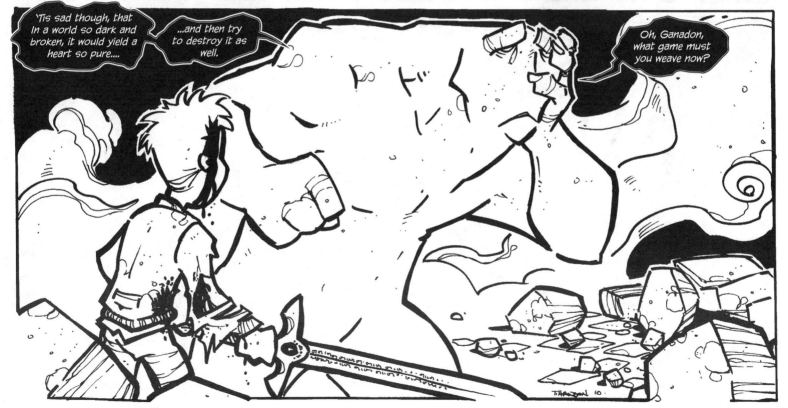

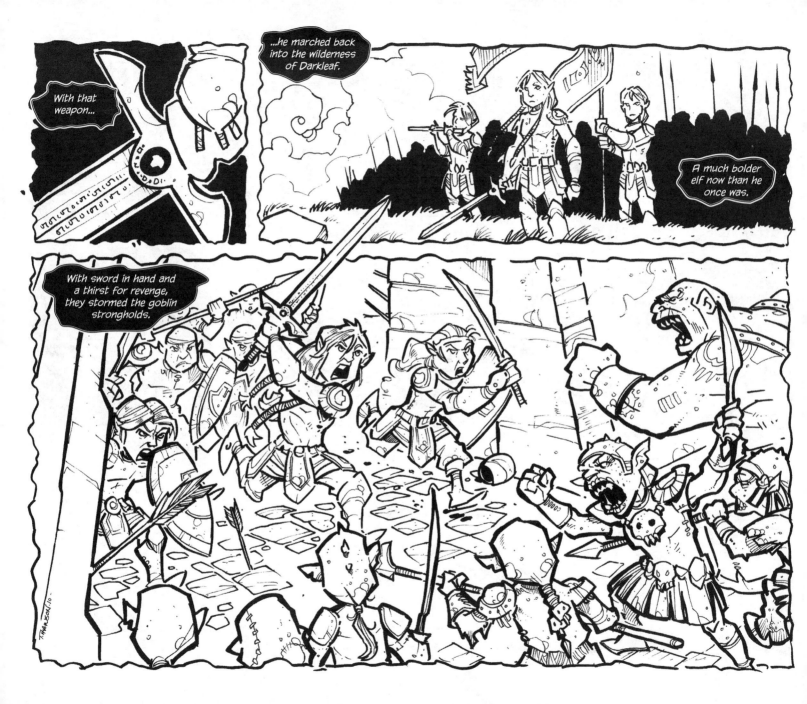

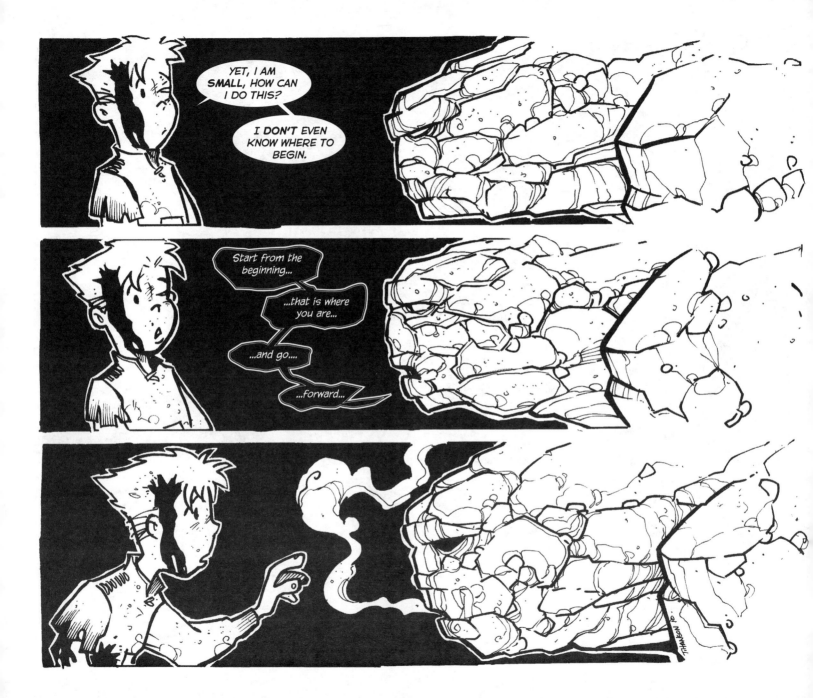

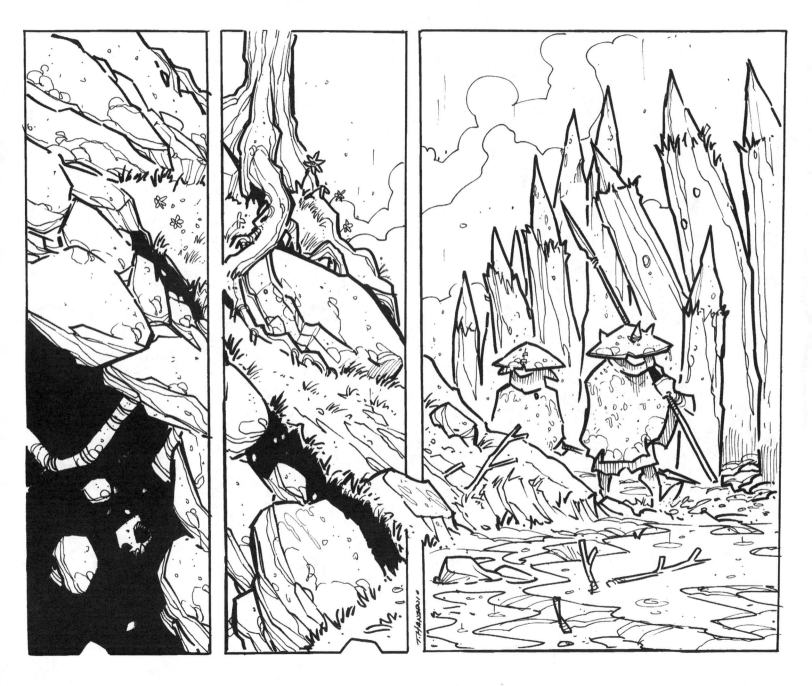

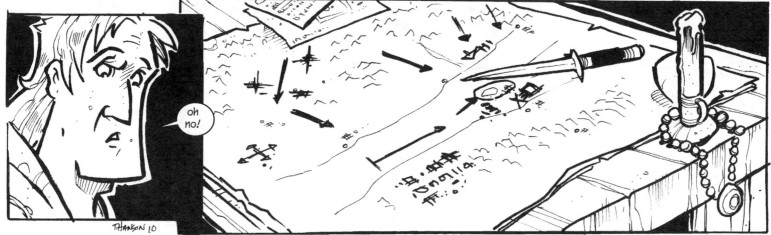

WE HAVE *TAKEN* THE TOWNS OF *GOLDENLEAF* AND *NINEBARK.*

AND THE OUTLYING FARMS?

TAKEN AS WELL, BADGER. *NOTHING* HAS SURVIVED.

WE HAVE HAD THE ELEMENT OF *COMPLETE* SURPRISE.

DO NOT BE OVER CONFIDENT, CAPTAIN. THE MUD PUSHERS CAN BE A HARD LOT TO DEAL WITH.

WE *MUST* KEEP PUSHING TOWARDS THE RIVER. MUCH DEPENDS ON OUR FORCES TO *ACHIEVE* THE GOALS OF THE BEAST KING HIMSELF.

LIKE ME, HE DOES NOT TOLERATE FAILURES.

NOW, *WHAT* OF THE GOBLIN PATROL THAT WAS *SENT* UNDERGROUND? THE BEAST KING *DEMANDS* TO KNOW.

THEY HAVE *NOT* RETURNED, SIR.

THERE ARE *MANY MYSTERIES* UNDERGROUND AND THEY *COULD* BE DELAYED.

I'M *NOT* INTERESTED ABOUT ANCIENT TALES USED TO *SCARE* GOBLIN WHELPS.

THAT MISSION *FROM* THE BEAST KING IS *CLEAR*. FIND THE TOMB AND *RETURN* WITH THE WEAPON.

IF THEY RETURN NOT, SEND A HUMAN SQUAD.

YOU *NEED* MORE FAITH IN MY TROOPS.

THEY *WILL* RETURN.

TO BE CONTINUED...

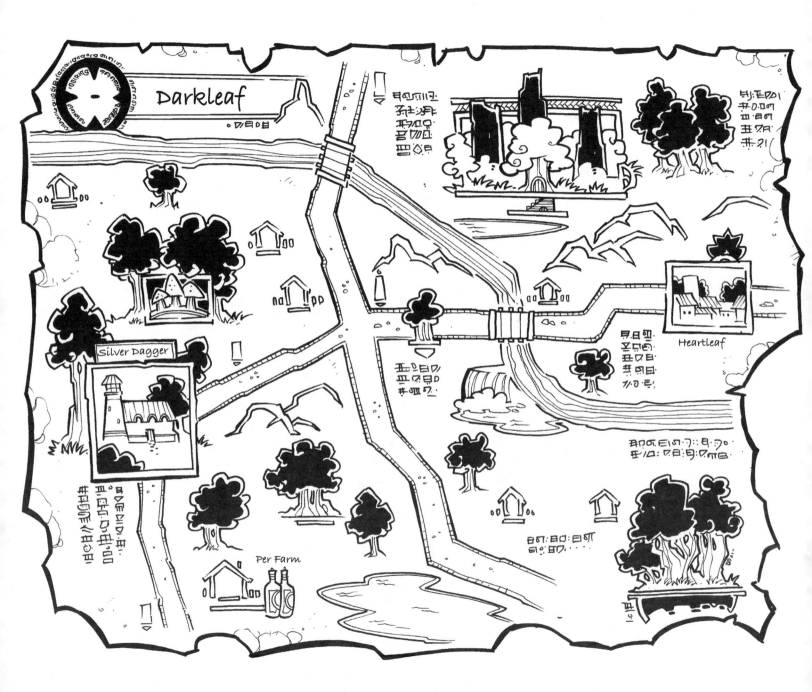

the Forest of Darkleaf

The forest of Darkleaf spans from the Northern Troll Mountains all the way to the Southern Mountains. It can take months to travel from the south to the north due to it's great size. It is an ancient forest of the world of the Broken Moon, but over the centuries it has changed greatly. Different civilizations have come and gone and staked their claims in the forest.

The forest has hosted many nations above and below ground. Underground, the Earthdwellers and Red Rock Trolls built huge complex cities and tunnel systems. Ogres, Elves, and Men worked the soil on the surface. For the most part, these great kingdoms lived in isolation and peace from one another. Something happened though and war came causing the great civilizations of Darkleaf to fall into ruin.

Three hundred years before our tale, a great war ripped through the forest. The Goblin nations started the war; they were looking to expand their territory. The fight led to the near annihilation of the Red Rock Trolls and the Ogres. During this dark time, the Earthdwellers fled south to the base of the river and formed new communities. The armies of Elves and Men were pushed back to the White Hall. Eventually they were able to switch to the offensive and push the Goblins back to the mountains.

The civilizations that had once thrived are nothing more than memories. The forest has since healed. Many farm communities have sprung up in Darkleaf. They are inhabited by the grandchildren of the Earthdwells and the humans of the forest. They live quiet lives, away from the large cities and politics that have developed up the river. Each year, they still pay an annual tribute to the White Hall.

the Silver Dagger

Deep within the forest of Darkleaf lies a small inn. Built around 250 years before our story, the Silver Dagger has gone through numerous repairs and upkeep. It was first owned by a human family, but in a game of chance, ownership changed hands. Two ogre brothers named Gort and Groggle became the new owners. They have run the inn for the last 35 years.

The inn is a two story dwelling in the shape of an L. It has a main hall and several common sleeping rooms upstairs. For the discriminating traveler, there are a few private rooms as well. Of course, they come at a price. The tower of the inn is split between storage and living quarters for part of the staff. The main kitchen is on the ground floor; the stoves here fuel the pipes to warm the entire hovel. Off the kitchen, a storeroom leads to the basement. Groggle brews most of his creations down there, and the Ogres dwell in the basement too. Rumor is that treasure is hidden under the inn, but those stories haven't been verified.

Set meal times are posted on the wall, but drinks are available any time. Payment for lodging and meals is taken when service is rendered. In the main hall, you join in games of chance but keep an eye on your goods. There have been whispers of a ghost that runs off with unwatched valuables.

Thank you to the following people who made this dream possible. I could not have done this without your support.

Helen Tanner
Alfred Moscola
Amy Ratcliffe
Bena Niemeyer
Bindi Boyce
Brian
Brian & Ariel Lloyd
Calissa Anne Moore
Capt. Kevin Noles IV
Charles St. John Smith III
Chris Grine
Christopher Daley
Dacy & Amy Nottingham
Daniel & Kelsey Butler
Darné and Christopher Lang
David 'Bub' Strainer
Dennis Wade Wolf, Sr.
Dylan
Dylan Mueller
Ervin Brubaker
Gabriel Garcia
Grandma Halina Kadziolka
Harald Demler
Howe Family

Jason Farrell
JD Calderon
Jewlian Harges
Jones Family
Josh Maher
Jun Lim
Kale Engelkemier
Ken Malidore
Kenneth Andersen - Kehaan
Lawrence Gill
Libbi Rich
Lon Braidwood
Martin Family
Matthew A. Scofield
Meleah Bryan
Michael Van Biesbrouck
Nich Wattanasin
Peter Denike
Phil Wait
Rick "@Fungible" Castello
Roy Sutton
Rusty Rowley
Sam Peacock
Scott King

Simon & Katherine Dent
Stephanie, Kevin & Malik
Stephen Crawford
Stephen Edwards
Stephen W. Kern
Steve Tracy
Susan Ator
The Bain Family
The Haddy Family
Tim Rogers
Todd Yerian
Vic Briseno
Eric Arsenault
Rachel Clark
Kevin Pointer
Chris Rich
Paul Roman Martinez
Terrana Cliff
Scott Head
Alvin Chan
Michael Rutter
Karen Sterling
Chris
Carson
Wesley_Stevens
David Sidore
Michael Jacob
daniel Shultz
Dr. Small
Joshua Sloan
Kelly Hoolihan
Leonardo Soledad
Christian DiGiacomo

Robert Lilley
Owen Ryan
Addy Van Ladesteijn
Amber Lanagan
Sebastian Wittenstein
Curtis Bates
Johnny Splendor
Glenn Craig
Abby Hanson
Michael Lerner
Trenton Wynter Brown
Ben Meginnis
Bryan Newton
Joshua
Cynthia Wood
Niels Weiglin Knudsen
Alan Gerding
Andy & Danielle Goldman
Aunt June
Austin Alldredge
Bahrtzoo
Beck "Tex Rimjob" Pascoe
Benjamin Bliss
Bob and Tiffany
Charles Sarratt
Christopher and Destiny Wayne
Christopher Burns
Daniel Keegan
Darren Parker
David Bolick
Diana Mom
Don
Dylan Kurtz

Eileen Walsh
Fergus Maximus
Filipe Sousa
Finn and Kirra
Heidi Berthiaume & Bud the Bunny
Jeff Cummins
Josie & her wonderful children
Keely Grant
Keirabean
Kellie Rupard-Schorr
Kieran and Cameron Fisk
Kim B.
Kim Tyler
Lev Trachtenberg
Liam Simmons
Marc D. Long
Matthew Grant
Michael R Howard
Niall and Finn Pocock
Paul Joseph Smoogen
Peter Teichroeb
Raevyn Fletcher
Rob Fullmer
Scott Kinoshita
Stacey Family
The Considine Family
The McKinley's
The Phipps Family
Willow Burr
Zolgar
chris tanaka
Arul Isai Imran
Jonathan Hepburn
Erin Hewett
StevenM

Bill Berry
Chip & Katie
Anticia
Rick Higginson
JÃ¸rn Nordli
Julia Fish
Mark Fugate
ttibke
Edmund Widl
Sanne Muurling
Jerry fredrickson
Chris Wilson
Timothy Brown
Arlene Zeller
Dan Sudkamp
Navin Isaiah
Aaron Miller
Derek Anderson
Patrick Coleman
Jens Bejer Pedersen
Ben Whittenbury
Adam J. Monetta
Justine
Mitch Hawkins
Stephen Cook
Al Kato
Jedai
Alec Mika
Bernard Lane
Brenna Lundquist
Callum and Beckett Rohrer
Ian Whiteside
Jacob Elias
Jeff Bolkovatz
Michael D. Johas Teener

Molly and Will McCarthy
Nathan Wanlass
Ross Demma
Shawn Demumbrum
Steven Bell
The Boudrie Family
Theresa and Ron Smith
Vega Family
Aaron Chandler
Jonathon MacKenzie
Christian Bunes-Roa
Erik W. Charles
Noel Burns
Ryan Campbell
Andrew Wilson
Ayal Pinkus
Brandon Klassen
Brenda Meitzler Anderson
Christopher Martin Beck
Georg Grosse-Hohl
Hari Ganesh Kumar
James Bucky Carter
Jordan Wayne Francis
Joshua Beale
Katherine & Elizabeth Rowe
Klaus Gottbehüt
L. M. May & Stephen Smoogen
Murray Wood
Nina and Mona Nakai-Strohsahl
Rod and Cindy Scollard
Sal Aldana
Saxony Scott
The Radul Family
The Trinidad Family
The Van Hoosier family

Franck Yvonnet
Samuel Basa
Chris Young
Ray Hill
Michael Carson
Scott Hanson
Sian Harrop
David Plotsky
Brandy, Travis and Ashley
Kuschel
Brian Juhl Devon Rampe & Family
Malin "Ravna" Runsten
Tony W. Liang
Laura
Dusty Averett
Sabia
Cathy
Joe Fuscaldo
John Morris
Julie Frost
Dave & Xephyr Inkpen
Mike Cachat
Matt Solberg
JoAnne George
Andrew C. "Lionheart" Overton
Tim Baker

Travis Hanson-
Is an Eisner nominated illustrator with a huge imagination. Travis spends his time in Southern California, with his lovely wife Janell, 5 children, a cat, one gecko and a psychotic clown fish.